A Robbie Reader

Meet Our New Student From

INDIA

Khadija Ejaz

Mitchell Lane

P.O. Box 196

Co..com

Meet Our New Student From

Australia • China • Colombia • Great Britain
• Haiti • **India** • Israel • Japan • Korea • Malaysia •
Mali • Mexico • New Zealand • Nicaragua • Nigeria
• Quebec • South Africa • Tanzania • Zambia •
Going to School Around the World

PUBLISHER'S NOTE: The facts on which the story
in this book is based have been thoroughly
researched. Documentation of such research
can be found on page 44. While every possible
effort has been made to ensure accuracy, the
publisher will not assume liability for damages
caused by inaccuracies in the data, and
makes no warranty on the accuracy of the
information contained herein.

To reflect current usage, we have chosen to
use the secular era designations BCE
("before the common era") and CE ("of the
common era") instead of the traditional
designations BC ("before Christ") and AD
(*anno Domini*, "in the year of the Lord").

**Library of Congress Cataloging-in-Publication
Data**

Ejaz, Khadija.
  Meet our new student from India / by Khadija
Ejaz.
      p. cm. — (A Robbie reader. Meet our new
student from)
  Includes bibliographical references and
index.
  ISBN 978-1-58415-779-3 (library bound)
  1. India—Juvenile literature. I. Title.
  DS407.E39 2009
   954—dc22
                                          2009001122

Printing   1   2   3   4   5   6   7   8   9
                                                    PLB

CONTENTS

India

One of the great wonders of the world, the Taj Mahal in Agra is probably the most well-known building in India. The total cost of construction of the mausoleum has been estimated to be trillions of today's American dollars.

Exciting News!

Chapter 1

"We're going to have a new student!" announced Mr. Shields as he walked to the front of his classroom at Avalon Elementary. His third-grade students dropped their pencils and excitedly turned to their teacher.

Colleen Turner raised her hand. "Who is the new student?" she asked.

Mr. Shields smiled. "Jai Singh will join us next week," he told the class, "and we're going to have a little welcome party for our new Indian student on his first day."

"Indian?" Colleen said. "Do you mean Native American?"

Mr. Shields shook his head. "I mean he is coming all the way from India!"

The students gasped. India! That was really far away, and they had never had a classmate from India before.

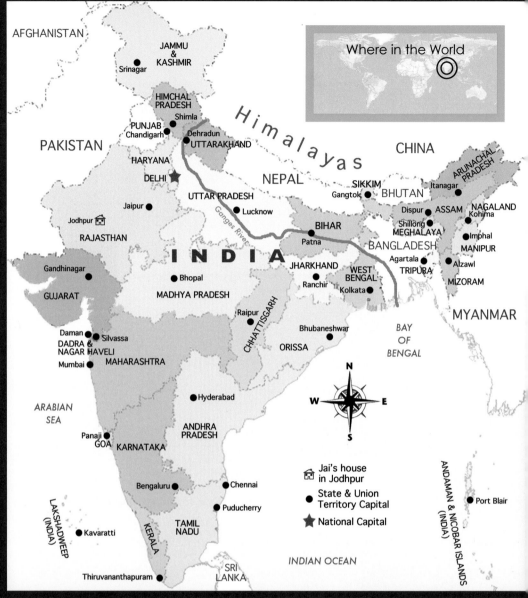

FACTS ABOUT INDIA

India Total Area:
2,000,000 square miles
(3.22 million square kilometers)

Population:
1.15 billion (July 2008 estimate)

Capital City:
New Delhi

Monetary Unit:
Indian Rupee

Religions:
Hinduism, Islam, Christianity, Sikhism,
Buddhism, Jainism, Zoroastrianism, Judaism

Ethnic Groups:
Indo-Aryan, Dravidian, others

Languages:
Hindi, Bengali, Telugu, Marathi, Tamil, Urdu,
Gujarati, Malayalam, Kannada, Oriya,
Punjabi, Assamese, Kashmiri, Sindhu, and
Sanskrit; English is the secondary language

Chief Exports:
Petroleum products, textile goods, gems
and jewelry, engineering goods, chemicals,
leather goods

fun FACTS

The Indian national flag is called the Tricolour because it has three colors in its design. Saffron (golden orange) stands for courage and sacrifice, white stands for peace and truth, and green stands for faith and chivalry. The blue central wheel or chakra has twenty-four spokes and is taken from a famous Ashoka pillar. It is the "wheel of law" that teaches life comes from action, while death is the result of inaction. Each spoke stands for a virtue, such as love, courage, and kindness.

Mr. Shields pulled down a map of the world. "I know we are all very excited about Jai, so I want us to learn more about where he is coming from." He pointed to the United States of America on the left side of the map. "This is where we are," he said, tapping Oklahoma. Then he walked over to the other side of the large map and pointed to a triangular country under China. "This," he said, "is where India is!" The students looked on with wide eyes.

Mr. Shields continued. "India is nearly on the opposite side of the world from us, in the continent of Asia. To get to America, Jai will have to travel by air for almost a day! See how many countries lie between India and America? Jai even has to fly over the Atlantic Ocean."

Tommy raised his hand and said, "Mr. Shields, my parents say that a lot of our jobs have gone to India."

Mr. Shields nodded. "That is true," he said. "The United States is India's largest trading partner, and India helps us save a lot of money by doing a lot of work for us in their country. This is called out-sourcing."

Outsourcing (OUT-sor-sing) was a new word for most of the students, so Mr. Shields wrote it on the board. He began to explain the idea with an example. "Sometimes when your parents have a

Indians have relied on elephants since ancient times. Elephants were used to fight during battle and are still used for transportation. They also became important religious symbols. Lord Ganesha, a Hindu god, is represented with the head of an elephant and body of a man.

question about something like a computer or a bank account, they will call a phone number for help. The phone call is answered in an office in India, where an English-speaking Indian person will help your parents with their question. This is easy to do because of computers and the Internet."

Colleen raised her hand. "So they speak English in India?"

"Yes, they do," Mr. Shields replied. "That's a good question, Colleen, thank you. India was once ruled by Great Britain, just as the colonies in North America were before they became the United States. That is how English was introduced to India."

Mr. Shields explained that in the upcoming week, the students would learn about India so that they would be ready for Jai when he arrived. Colleen couldn't wait to get started. She already had all sorts of ideas for the party they were planning for him. Jai would love it!

Stone Bronze Buddha Statue, Delhi Museum

India

One of the many pillars set up by Ashoka 5,000 years ago, the one at Vaishali bears a single lion which faces north, the direction Buddha traveled on his last journey. Excavations suggest that a Buddhist monastery once flourished at this site.

The Oldest Continuous Civilization

Chapter 2

The land that is now India has a long history of empires and kingdoms and changing borders. Many modern countries around India, including Pakistan, Afghanistan, and Nepal, share India's ancient history. Civilization there can be traced back all the way to 2500 BCE, to the Indus River Valley. The people of this civilization were known for their advanced **irrigation** and agricultural trade practices. The ruins of the Indus cities of Harappa and Mohenjo-Daro can still be seen in the area around the Indus.

India was a center of great education and learning. The world's first university was established in Takshashila in 700 BCE. Important developments in math, such as trigonometry (trih-guh-NAH-muh-tree)—the beauty in the numbers behind triangles—and the decimal system, were invented in India. Indian scientist Aryabhatta invented the number zero and proved that Earth revolves around the sun.

The belief system called yoga was also developed in India.

Sometime around 2000 BCE, the Aryan people arrived in India from the northwest and settled in the Ganga (or Ganges) River Valley. This period is known as the Vedic period because that's when the Vedas, the sacred texts of the Hindus, were written.

Vedic society was divided into four **castes**: Brahmins (priests), Kshatriyas (warriors), Vaishyas (traders), and Shudras (laborers). They also divided life into four phases of 25 years each: Brahmacharya (for education), Grihastha (for marriage and family), Vanaprastha (for abandoning worldly pleasures), and Sanyasa (for meditation in isolation). This system still influences Indian life today.

Aryabhatta

By the fourth century CE, Chandragupta Maurya had united most of what is modern India under the Maurya **dynasty**.

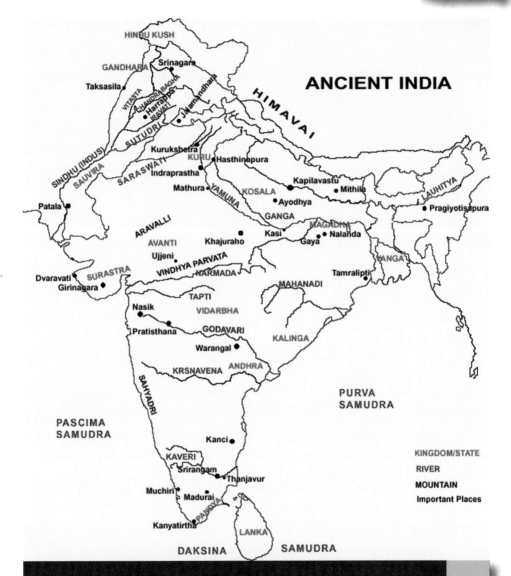

ANCIENT INDIA

The modern country called India has existed for a little over 60 years. The region, however, has been home to numerous kingdoms that rose and fell over thousands of years. The kingdoms described in the ancient Sanskrit epics, the Ramayana and the Mahabharata, form what is called the Epic phase of Indian history.

The Mauryas ruled India for 150 years. The last and greatest of all Maurya emperors, Ashoka, is well known for changing his religion from the Vedic beliefs of his time to Buddhism. He set up Buddhist symbols such as the pillars of love and peace throughout his empire. The emblem of India—the four lions, called the Sarnath Lion Capital—is taken from one of those pillars.

After the decline of the Mauryas, India was divided once again. The Gupta dynasty ushered in the Golden Age in northern India. Great advances were made in art, literature, science, and government. During this time, various kingdoms also flourished in South India.

In the tenth and eleventh centuries, armies from Turkey and Afghanistan invaded India. They established their kingdoms in Delhi. Over the next 700 years, their religion, Islam, became more and more popular in India.

In the sixteenth century, the Turk Babar became the first Mughal emperor to rule North India. Over the next 200 years, the Mughal emperors would influence South India as well. Some of these emperors were Shah Jahan, Akbar, and Aurangezeb. The Taj Mahal, one of the wonders of the world, was built by Shah Jahan in memory of his wife, Mumtaz Mahal.

Europeans began to sail to India after Vasco da Gama, a Portuguese explorer, discovered the first water route to India in 1498. They would no longer have to cross the towering Himalayas to trade for the spices and silk that India had to offer. Britain opened its first **outpost** in South Asia at Surat in 1619. By the 1700s, the British East India Company controlled a large portion of India.

The Indians, who wanted **independence** (in-dee-PEN-dents) from the British Empire, launched the Revolt of 1857. Although the rebellion failed, the British East India Company no longer ruled in India—but Britain still did. In 1877, Queen Victoria of England assumed the title Empress of India.

Artist John Wood's rendition of a British East India Company ship approaching Bombay, India, in the 1850s. At first, the British company wanted to trade with India. Over time, the English used military power to increase profit and rule over the people.

Over the next many years, leaders such as Jawaharlal Nehru, Mohandas Karamchand Gandhi, Subhash Chandra Bose, Bhagat Singh, and Maulana Abul Kalam Azad led the Indian struggle for freedom.

Jawaharlal Nehru (front left) was the first Prime Minister of India, and was also an important political figure during the fight for an independent India against the British Empire. Indians celebrate his birthday, November 14, as Children's Day because of his belief in the value of young people. It is for this reason that Indians often refer to him as Chacha (uncle) Nehru. The Indian jacket he often wore, the sherwani, is also called a Nehru jacket in his honor.

Mohandas Karamchand Gandhi (right) is also known as Father of the Nation because of his important role in the freedom struggle against the British. Indians call him Gandhiji out of respect. Gandhi was born in South Africa and was a lawyer. After living in South Africa and seeing the unfair treatment of the people there, he joined the Indian freedom struggle.

On July 25, 2007, Pratibha Devisingh Patil (center) became the first female president of India. She succeeded Dr. A.P.J. Abdul Kalam. Dr. Kalam was a very popular president and highly respected for his work as an engineer in the fields of missile and rocket technology.

Finally, on August 15, 1947, India became a free nation. Jawaharlal Nehru became the prime minister. Pakistan, which was mostly Muslim, and the rest of India, which was mainly Hindu, became separate nations. The constitution of India went into effect on January 26, 1950, and established the country as a **sovereign**, **democratic republic**. It assures its citizens of justice, equality, and liberty. Each year, January 26 is celebrated as Republic Day.

India

The monsoon season brings both relief and difficulties to the people of the tropical country. While the rain replenishes the water supply and brings down the high temperature, the amount of rain often causes landslides, floods, and other natural disasters.

Land of the
Monsoon

Chapter **3**

India is the seventh largest country in the world and is about one-third the size of the United States. It is on the Indian **subcontinent** in Asia, and shares its border with many other countries, including Pakistan, Nepal, Bangladesh, Bhutan, Sri Lanka, Burma, and China. The southern portion of India is a **peninsula** (peh-NIN-suh-luh). It is bordered on three sides by water: the Arabian Sea on the west, the Indian Ocean on the south, and the Bay of Bengal in the east.

The country is divided into 28 states and 7 union territories, with New Delhi as the capital. Uttar Pradesh is the most densely populated state, and Mumbai (formerly called Bombay) is the largest city. Each state has its own unique languages, clothing, food, and art.

India's **terrain** varies widely from its northern borders to its southernmost tip. The Himalayas, the

highest and youngest mountain range in the world, are located in the north. The fertile Indo-Gangetic **plains** run south of the Himalayas. The river systems of the Ganges, the Indus, and the Brahmaputra all start in the Himalayas and run through these plains. Most of west India is covered by the Thar desert. In south India are the Deccan **plateau**, with the Western and Eastern Ghat mountains on either side. The oldest rock formations in the Deccan plateau are over a billion years old! India also has two **archipelagoes**: the Lakshadweep islands, which are made of coral, and the Andaman & Nicobar islands, formed by volcanoes.

The Hindus have long considered the waters of the Ganga (or Ganges) river sacred. The National River of India originates in the Himalayas and empties into the Bay of Bengal, spawning various tributaries along the way. Many Hindus yearn to wash their sins away by bathing in the Ganga at least once in their lifetime.

fun FACTS

Scientists believe that millions of years ago, the Indian subcontinent was part of a supercontinent called Pangaea. After drifting north and east for millions of years, the subcontinent collided with Eurasia. The site of their collision folded to form the Himalayan range. These huge pieces of land are still drifting together, pushing the Himalayas higher and causing earthquakes throughout Asia.

Most of India lies between the equator and the tropic of Cancer. The climate is greatly influenced by the terrain, especially by the Himalayas, which block the cold winds from the north and trap the moisture-laden warm winds from the south. These warm winds bring most of India's rain, which is called the monsoon.

India has four major seasons: dry, cool winter (December to February); dry, hot summer (March to May); southwest monsoon (June to September); and northeast monsoon (October and November). Cherrapunji is the only Indian city that gets rain in both monsoon seasons. It receives the highest amount of rainfall in the world—428 inches per year. (One year, it rained over 1,000 inches!)

Because of India's varied terrain and climate, many kinds of crops grow there, including wheat,

Rudyard Kipling probably had the Bengal tiger in mind when he came up with Shere Khan, the villainous tiger in his famous Jungle Book stories. The National Animal of India is an endangered species, and conservation organizations such as Project Tiger have been set up to protect it.

Farming in India provides the second highest farm output in the world. Agriculture is such an important part of the Indian economy that it plays a big role in the overall development of the country. Farmers are India's most precious resource.

rice, oilseeds, sugar, cotton, jute, potatoes, and tea. Over half of the jobs in India are in agriculture.

You can get a good idea of the diverse Indian wildlife from the Disney cartoon *The Jungle Book*, which was set entirely in the forests of India. Lions, tigers, monkeys, elephants, snakes, peacocks, and other exotic species live in India. Several types of animals, such as the royal Bengal tiger, Asiatic lion, and Indian rhinoceros, are considered endangered, and it is against the law to hunt them.

India

India's foundation is its villages, and it is these villages that essentially run the country's main industry—agriculture. Village life is simple, but its inhabitants work very hard. One can see the brilliant colors of village life when everyone in the community comes together to celebrate.

Unity in
Diversity

Chapter

India is the largest democracy in the world, with a population of over 1 billion, second only to China. Over thousands of years as the cultures have mixed, India has become a complex society with a mind-boggling variety of languages, art, fashion, music and dances, food, and customs.

Some people mistakenly think that India is home only to the Hindus who speak Hindi. In reality, India has one of the largest Muslim populations in the world. Indians might also be Christian, Sikh, Buddhist, Jain, Zoroastrian, Jewish, or from a tribal religion. Religion has always been very important in Indian society and politics. The religions practiced by 25 percent of the world—Hinduism, Buddhism, Jainism, and Sikhism—started in India.

India has only three national holidays: Independence Day (August 15), Republic Day (January 26), and Gandhi Jayanti (Gandhi's birthday—October 2). Indians are proud of their ancient history and

Shiva the Destroyer is the third god of the Hindu Trimurti (trinity). He is often depicted deep in **meditation** with a third eye on his forehead and a trident, his preferred weapon. Some say that the universe will end the day his third eye opens.

culture, and you can see it in the patriotic way they celebrate these holidays. The whole country joins in honoring those who fought for Independence by hosting parades in its cities and schools. Children take part in these celebrations by performing traditional dances and singing patriotic songs. Other Indian festivals—such as Diwali, Onam, Eid-ul-fitr, Christmas, and Buddha Jayanti—are religious in origin. Their observance varies by region, but they are generally celebrated by people of all beliefs. All this means a lot of holidays for the schoolchildren!

Hindi is the most widely understood and the national language of India, but there are 21 other official regional languages. These don't include more than 1,600 other local dialects that are spoken all over the country.

Top: Independence Day celebrations are a time when Indian people celebrate their dynamic culture and the spirit of the saffron, white, and green. It is a time of a great unity between all communities in India as they remember the sacrifices of those who set India free from the British Empire.

Below: Thousands flock to the famous Republic Day parade in New Delhi every year when India proudly displays its army, navy, and air force to its people and to the world. Similar parades are also held on a smaller scale in the capitals of individual states.

India has the world's largest English-speaking population. Indian English has a British style, but locals often mix it with their own language. For example, Hindi speakers might mix English and Hindi words while talking. This new style of English is called Hinglish.

Not all schools in India teach in the same language. Some schools teach in English. Most schools make their students learn Hindi, but that is not the case in some areas.

Education is very important in India. It is not unusual to see students studying all day and taking extra coaching classes in the evenings. Knowledge and books are considered sacred, and teachers are given as much respect as one's parents. All schools have their own uniforms.

Dance and music are also very important to Indians. A lot of children are trained in classical dances. Some of these are Kathak, Bharatnatyam, and Kuchipudi. They are also trained in music, such as North Indian Hindustani music and South Indian

Children in India come from different ethnic backgrounds but they go to school and play together. All schools in India have their own uniforms, and they are strict about these dress codes. Children are taught to respect their teachers and work hard, but they are also encouraged to take part in school activities like sports, debating, and art and science shows.

Carnatic music. India's love for the arts shows in its movies. Its Hindi film industry is lovingly called Bollywood because it is like California's Hollywood but is based in the city that used to be called Bombay. Most Indian movies have a lot of songs and dances in them, and children enjoy watching them with their families and friends.

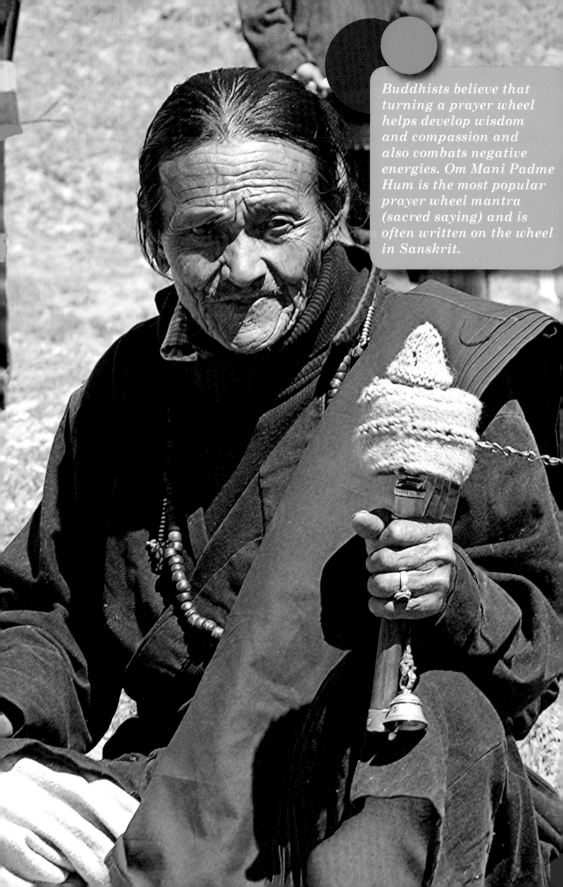

Buddhists believe that turning a prayer wheel helps develop wisdom and compassion and also combats negative energies. Om Mani Padme Hum is the most popular prayer wheel mantra (sacred saying) and is often written on the wheel in Sanskrit.

Indian life is simple and conservative (kon-SER-vuh-tiv). Most people live in **joint families**, but in bigger cities like Delhi and Calcutta, people have started living in **nuclear families** like they do in America. Children are respectful of their elders, and the elders are expected to be kind and loving to the children. Grown-ups take care of their elderly parents and often have them live with them.

The style of clothing varies all over the country, depending on the climate and religion, but almost everywhere people dress **modestly**. The men usually wear long qurtas (shirts) with dhotis or pajamas. Women dress in shalwar qameezes or saris, or in their local style of clothing. People do wear Western outfits, but that is more common in the larger cities.

You can find a wide variety of food in India. People in the north include a lot more bread in their diet, while the people in the south use more rice and pulses instead. East Indians eat mostly fish and rice. West Indian food is generally vegetarian and milk-based. Chicken and fish are the most common meats eaten in India. Indian food is known for being spicy, and many a foreigner has been pleasantly surprised by the delicious mix of masalas (spices) in their very first bite. You can try some of these dishes at Indian restaurants in your area.

The national game of India is field hockey, and soccer, tennis, and chess are also quite popular. But nothing gets the nation going like cricket! India has

Indian food is delicious! Have you ever had chicken tikka, chicken makhani, qorma, or beef kebabs with parathas? How about some vegetable pulao with a side of yogurt? Be careful because Indian food can be spicy!

one of the best cricket teams in the world. It regularly plays against other world giants, like England, Australia, West Indies, Pakistan, Sri Lanka, New Zealand, and South Africa. Other sports that children often play in India are kabaddi, kho-kho, and gilli-danda. Some historians believe that cricket originated from gilli-danda. Gilli-danda is a simpler form of

Future members of the world-famous Indian cricket team are formed on the streets, where young boys and girls spend hours perfecting their batting, bowling, and fielding strategies. The most popular sport in the nation, cricket sets emotions ablaze during matches—much like soccer does in Europe.

cricket where two sticks, a short gilli and a longer danda, are used instead of a ball and bat.

Even more famous than sports figures, though, is Mohandas Karamchand Gandhi. His belief in changing harsh British rule without violence greatly influenced other heroes, such as Martin Luther King Jr. and Nelson Mandela. Actor Ben Kingsley played Gandhi in a famous movie about his life. Ask your local library for the movie *Gandhi* to learn more about this famous freedom fighter.

India

Jai reflects his country's colorful heritage in the clothes he wears. Bright colors symbolize life, happiness, and everything good to Indians. The country can get very hot, so people usually wear cotton.

Namaste, Jai!

Chapter 5

Colleen and her classmates had spent all week learning about India. Today, they had dressed in the colors of the Indian flag and had decorated the walls with pictures of India. They'd even brought in a sound track of a famous Bollywood movie for everyone to dance to. Mr. Shields had prepared mango lassis for everyone.

Jai Singh shyly entered the classroom with his parents. His mother was wearing a colorful sari decorated with small mirrors, and she smiled at the diyas the children had placed at the classroom door. Jai's father wore a long bright orange shirt, a *qurta*, and a smart pair of spotless white cotton pants. He even wore a big orange **turban**. Jai was dressed like his father except that he had on a smaller raspberry-colored cloth hat.

Colleen approached Jai with a smile. "I like your hat, Jai!" she said. "Is that from Arabia? It looks like hats I've seen in Aladdin."

Mr. Singh laughed. "It's a turban," he corrected Colleen. "In Rajasthan, the state where we're from, turbans are a common headdress for men. It's actually a single long piece of cloth that's wrapped around our head. The size of a person's turban can tell you a lot about his social status." Mr. Singh smiled. "We are not from Arabia at all!"

Mr. Shields started playing the Bollywood CD, and Jai started tapping his feet. "That's my favorite song from the movie!" he exclaimed. "My dad, grandfather, and I play sarangis together in our spare time. They are a little like your violin, and it's a lot of fun."

The rest of the children ran up to the Singh family to say hello. Jai and his parents were very happy to hear the children greet them in Hindi. They even enjoyed the mango lassi Mr. Shields had started serving.

ENGLISH	HINDI
Greetings	Namaste (nuh-MUS-tay)
Please	Kripiya (KRIP-yaa)
Thank you	Dhanyawaad (DHUN-yuh-waad)
Yes	Ji haan (JEE hann)
No	Ji naheen (JEE nuh-heen)

"How do you like Tulsa so far?" Colleen asked Jai.

"I miss my friends and the rest of my family," he told her. "We used to live with my grandmother in our family's old brick home in Jodhpur. It had a courtyard, and we even had a hand-operated

Jai enjoys playing the sarangi with his father and grandfather. Meaning "a hundred colors," the sarangi is one of the most difficult instruments to play. Some say that the music from a sarangi sounds like the human voice.

water pump. All my friends lived nearby. The houses are very different here, and I don't have anyone to play with yet."

"Why did you move?" Colleen asked.

Jai's mother holds his brother Abhay and poses for a picture with his sister Preethi, along with their friends and relatives. Jai's family lived in a joint family system in India, and he misses his grandmother and neighbors who formed his community.

"I got a scholarship to study in America," said Jai, blushing slightly, "and so my father, mother, brother Abhay, and sister Preethi moved here together. My father will be teaching traditional Rajasthani music at the University of Oklahoma."

"My mom works there too!" Colleen exclaimed. "Maybe we can all go to the college football games in the late winter."

Jai's hometown is also called the Blue City. Jodhpur, the second largest city in Rajasthan, earned its nickname from its famous blue-tinged whitewashed houses. Along the same lines, Jaipur, the state capital, is known as the Pink City.

"American football!" said Jai, his dark eyes sparkling. "I have always wanted to learn about it! My brother and I also often play football, but football in India is actually like America's soccer."

"Do you play in the snow in India?" asked Colleen.

"No. Rajasthan is in the Thar desert, and it never gets cold enough to snow there. It only shows on the tallest mountains in other parts of India, which I've never seen," said Jai.

"Oh, don't worry," Colleen said, putting her arm around Jai's shoulder. "Snow is great. It's so much fun making snowmen and having snowball fights. Do you know what a snow angel is? We'll show you how to make one!"

"That would be great," Jai said excitedly. "First I have some pictures to show you that I brought from home."

Jai smiled, and Colleen's heart warmed. She had been feeling bad that he had left all his friends behind in India. Mr. Shields had also been worried about the difficulties Jai might have while adjusting to his new life in Tulsa. But after the wonderful reception the Singh family had received from the students, Colleen knew that Jai would have nothing to worry about. Shy Jai was already feeling at home at Avalon Elementary.

Things You Will Need

An adult

Glasses

Blender

Teaspoon

Spoon

Ingredients

3 glasses of yogurt

1 glass crushed ice

1 glass ripe mango pieces or pulp

Sugar to taste or unsweetened
   fruit juice or pulp

Chocolate and/or
   vanilla ice cream

A dollop of whipped cream

1 teaspoon slivered almonds

How To Make

Mango Lassi

Instructions

1. With the help of an ADULT, put the yogurt, mango, ice, and sugar, juice, or pulp in a blender and blend until smooth.

2. Pour into glasses.

3. Top with ice cream, a dollop of whipped cream, and slivered almonds.

4. Serve.

Make Your Own
Diwali Diya

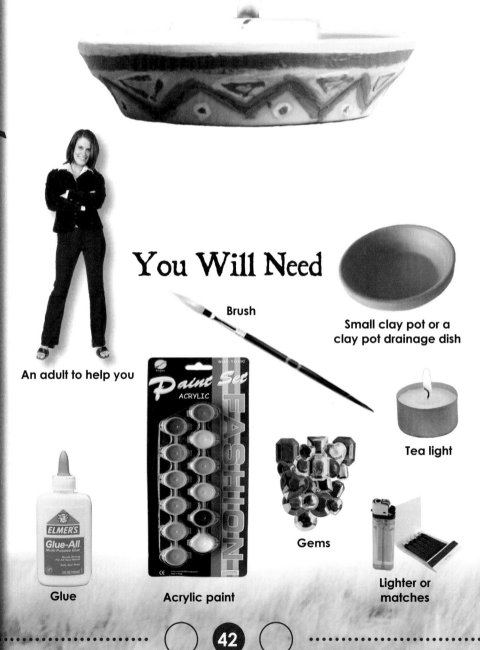

You Will Need

Brush

Small clay pot or a clay pot drainage dish

An adult to help you

Paint Set ACRYLIC — NON-TOXIC — FASHION

Tea light

Gems

Glue — ELMER'S Glue-All Multi-Purpose Glue

Acrylic paint

Lighter or matches

Diwali is the Hindu Festival of Lights, which celebrates the return of Lord Rama, a good and mighty king, from his exile to his home in Ayodhya. The residents of Ayodhya marked his return by lighting diyas all over the city. Hindus still follow this Diwali tradition. Welcome guests in your home by making this pretty little diya.

Instructions for Making a Diwali Diya

1. Paint a bright design on a clay pot or clay pot drainage dish.

2. When the paint is dry, decorate the pot by gluing on gems and little mirrors if you want.

3. When the glue is dry, place a tealight inside the pot.

4. **Have an adult** help you light the tealight and put it in a safe place.

Further Reading

Books

Chatterjee, Manini, and Anita Roy. *India*. New York: Dorling Kindersley, 2002.

Dalal, A. Kamala. *Countries of the World: India*. Washington, D.C.: National Geographic Society, 2007.

Flatt, Lizann. *Country Files: India*. North Mankato, Minnesota: Smart Apple Press, 2003.

Jermyn, Leslie, and Radhika Srinivasan. *Cultures of the World: India*. New York: Benchmark Books, 2002.

Moseley, James. *The Ninth Jewel of the Mughal Crown: The Birbal Tales from the Oral Traditions of India*. Pasadena, California: Summerwind Marketing, 2001.

Swan, Erin Pembrey. *India*. Danbury, Connecticut: Children's Press, 2002.

Works Consulted

This book is based on the author's knowledge and experience as an Indian. She was born in Lucknow, India, and raised in Muscat, Sultanate of Oman. Other sources she used are listed below.

Blackwell, Fritz. *India: A Global Studies Handbook*. Santa Barbara: ABC-CLIO, 2004.

McLeod, John. *The History of India*. Westport, Connecticut: Greenwood Press, 2002.

New York Life: Facts About India http://www.newyorklife.com/cda/0,3254,13042,00.html

US Department of State: Bureau of South and Central Asian Affairs October 2007, "Background Note: India" http://www.state.gov/r/pa/ei/bgn/3454.htm

Wolpert, Stanley. *India*. Berkley: University of California Press, 1991.

Wood, Michael. *India*. New York: Basic Books, 2007.

On the Internet

Bawarchi: Indian Food Recipes and Cuisine
http://www.bawarchi.com

Bollywood: India's Film Industry
http://www.bollywood.com

Incredible India
http://www.incredibleindia.org

Further Reading

Maps of India
   http://www.mapsofindia.com
The Times of India
   http://www.timesofindia.com

Embassy
Embassy of India, Washington, DC
2107 Massachusetts Avenue, NW
Washington, D.C. 20008
Tel: (202) 939-7000
Fax: (202) 265-4351
http://www.indianembassy.org

India 1 rupee

India 1000 rupee—front
(top); back (right)

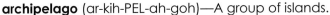

archipelago (ar-kih-PEL-ah-goh)—A group of islands.

Buddhism (BOO-dizm)—A religion of eastern and central Asia that grew out of the teaching of Gautama Buddha.

caste (KAST)—A division of society based on differences of wealth, inherited rank or privilege, profession, occupation, or race.

democratic (deh-muh-KRAA-tik)—Governed by the people.

dynasty (DY-nes-tee)—A line of rulers from the same family.

epic (EH-pik)—A long poem telling of heroic deeds.

Hinduism (HIN-doo-izm)—The dominant religion of India, which involves the worship of many gods and belief in reincarnation (being reborn on earth after death).

independence (in-dee-PEN-dents)—Freedom from control or influence of others.

irrigation (eer-ih-GAY-shun)—A system for watering farmland.

Jainism (JAA-ih-nizm)—A religion of India originating in the sixth century BCE and teaching liberation of the soul by right knowledge, right faith, and right conduct.

joint family—An entire family, including grandparents, aunts, uncles, and cousins.

mausoleum (mah-zuh-LEE-um)—A large building for housing tombs.

meditation (meh-dih-TAY-shun)—A state of calm and reflection of one's life.

modestly (MAH-dest-lee)—Conforming to standards of proper behavior, good taste, or morality.

nuclear family—The part of a family that is just one set of parents and their children.

outpost—A military base established in another country by treaty or agreement.

peninsula (peh-NIN-suh-lah)—A piece of land that is nearly surrounded by water.

plain (PLAYN)—An area of level or rolling treeless country.

plateau (plah-TOH)—A large, flat area of land that is raised above the surrounding land.

republic (ree-PUB-lik)—A government whose leader is not a king or queen but who in modern times is usually a president.

Sikhism (SEEK-izm)—A religion of India founded about 1500 by Guru Nanak and marked by belief in one god and rejection of idolatry and caste.

sovereign (SAH-vren)—Independent.

subcontinent (sub-KON-tih-nent)—A major portion of a continent.

supercontinent (SOO-per-kon-tih-nent)—A huge landmass that scientists believe included many of the current continents.

terrain (tuh-RAYN)—The features of a piece of land.

turban (TER-bun)—A cap around which a long cloth is wound.

Index

ABOUT THE AUTHOR

Khadija Ejaz was born in Lucknow, India, and raised in Muscat, Sultanate of Oman. She earned her bachelor's and master's degrees in Computer Science and Management Information Systems at Oklahoma State University, Stillwater, and now lives between India, Oman, and Canada. A full-time IT professional, she freelances as a writer and has numerous writing credits to her name. Her other interests include filmmaking, acting, photography, volunteer work, and the theater.

To learn more about Khadija, visit her website at http://khadijaejaz.netfirms.com.